These are not my Dreams
Nothing Here is Purple

Michael Conley

Published by Nine Pens

2021

www.ninepens.co.uk

ISBN: 978-1-8384321-1-9

002

5   Baby Parade

6   For A Whole Week, The Tremendous Legislator Suffers From The Delusion That He's Made Of Balloons

7   The Little Robot Who Makes You Relax

8   The Tremendous Legislator Harbours A Brief Obsession With Helicopters

9   Necklace Of Ears

11   A Thrill

13   The Tremendous Legislator Has Insisted That Everything Be An Indescribable Shade Of Purple He Dreamed Once

15   Little Sociopath Attends The Wedding Reception Of A Distant Relative

16   At The Park, A Grown Man Has Got His Head Caught In The Railings

17   If You Want To Make Sense Of The Greatest Love Songs Ever Written

18   I Am So Angry With You For Bringing This Here

19   An Otherwise Uneventful Holiday

21   On A Spring Morning In April, The Newspaper Editor Makes Cupcakes With His Beautiful Son

23   The Tremendous Legislator Had A Wonderful Sense Of Humour

24   Trucks

25   Lobsters Make Noise Like Violins

27   The Tremendous Legislator's Second Most Accurate Body Double Is Torn To Pieces Attempting To Flee The City

28   These Are The Things You Can Do When You Sneak Into The Old Ice-Cream Factory Alone, After Midnight

29   The Tremendous Legislator Has Taken To Sniffing Petrol

30   The Moment When The Tremendous Legislator Should've Known The Jig Was Up

31   Branch

32   The Tremendous Legislator's Head Is Put On Display By The New Regime

33   Rat Centipede

34   These Three Young Ladies Have Come All The Way From Australia

What are you laughing at? You're laughing at yourselves!
                                        -Nikolai Gogol

Baby Parade

After Charles Simic

I hope you're enjoying your Baby Parade, babies!
I shouted as they paraded up and down.
We're not babies! the little girl yelled.
And it's not a Baby Parade! the little boy added.
It sure looked like a Baby Parade to me.

Where did they get off, these two, thinking
they could just have a parade whenever they chose to?
The little boy had found pink feathers to wear
and round, green-rimmed sunglasses.
The little girl had a blue plastic bugle. *Welcome*

welcome welcome to the big parade, she sang.
The dog was joining in, but not with enough focus
to be seriously considered a parade member.
All this, by the way, was contained within their front garden.
And that was the whole parade. Of course it was:

they didn't know anyone except their own parents.
What is this parade even in honour of? I asked,
but by this time they were ignoring me.
I watched, in disbelief, a little while longer.
Nice try, idiots, I whispered, shaking my head. *Nice try.*

For A Whole Week, The Tremendous Legislator Suffers From The Delusion He's Made Of Balloons

His first instinct is to tell no one.
He's covered in a layer of fine white dust and in the morning His head
bobs gently in the bathroom's convection currents.
His face has become a sadface emoji drawn on with marker pen.
In His suit, He is ninety percent more air than usual.
His arsehole is prodigiously dry and He fears everyone will hear it squeak.

The only option is to carry on, though when you're a man made of balloons,
everything is a needle: He avoids corkscrews, kettle-baked potato crisps
and hedgehogs; easy enough for Him with His life of smoothed edges
and soft fruits. He bounces down the marble stairs like an astronaut.
The Advisors say nothing; they still jump
at the helium cheep of His voice.

When one of them makes a mistake and says *Sir, I'm so sorry*
to have let You down,
He screeches out loud and spends the rest of the day in bed,
vibrating with rage at the thought that they're all laughing at Him.
This is the week He works harder than He's ever worked before.
He has all cats de-clawed, bans the sale of vampire teeth at Halloween,
and places big orders with a firm that makes those long inflatable buffers
that line bowling lane gutters, then has them installed along every motorway.

Road traffic deaths plummet to a historic low and the People sing His genius.
Then, inexplicably, He wakes up, all flesh and soft hair again.
He runs His hands over the fatty parts of Himself and lets His nails grow.
He considers getting a tattoo across His back: a huge, photorealistic image
of His own smiling face, His right hand doing a thumbs-up sign.

The Little Robot Who Makes You Relax

I am the little robot who makes you relax.
Take me into the bath with you:
I will splash you with my metal pincers
and repeat the word *relax* in a level tone
until you are completely relaxed.
The splashing, while unsettling at first,

will release tiny electrical impulses
that enter your pores through the water.
They are proven to slow heart rate
and reduce brain activity. Don't worry,
my pincers have rounded safety edges
and all of my moving parts are encased in rubber

so you will not be electrocuted.
Please do not use me to masturbate with:
that is not what I am for.

The Tremendous Legislator Harbours A Brief Obsession With Helicopters

What He's really good at
is replicating the sound of rotor blades
using His tongue, teeth and lips,
which He's started to do
throughout Cabinet briefings.
He has a plain black leather jacket
on the breast of which is a tiny picture
of a grinning cartoon helicopter
with big moist Disney eyes
and nobody knows where He got it.

Often when people get obsessed with things
they end up knowing lots about those things
but, truly, He knows nothing about helicopters.

He goes out every day
in the one we had custom-built:
the controls aren't connected to anything
and there's a secret compartment
in which the real pilot hides.

He's started wondering out loud
what someone's head would end up looking like
if they walked face-first into the whizzing bit,
so obviously that's going to have to be arranged
at some point. Still, for now

it all seems to be making Him happy;
He's started to refer to Himself
as the World's Sexiest Helicopter Pilot.

Necklace Of Ears

After Carolyn Forche

Granted, the child loves the necklace of ears you brought her
but we do have some questions:

                like when she asked
are these actual ears and you said *no of course not sweetheart*
and then you winked at us over her head:

                what did that mean?
She's refusing to take it off, even to sleep, even to bathe
and when challenged she says

                impossible, for within
is sealed the vestigial power of all my slaughtered foes
and she curls her little fist around one of the ears

                and looks past us
towards the sky. We're assuming you taught her to do that?
Before all this,

                she was afraid of the dustbin men
but now every Tuesday morning she charges bellowing
right into the jaws of their truck

                with her little cardboard sword
and she really does believe she would come off better.
We're afraid that the ears

                will have to go,
that they may be exerting a malign influence over her.
When we ask her,

                tucking her in at night,

Darling, do those things ever whisper terrifying incantations
in the dark?

O precious one, do they
spit cold imperatives to evil while you sleep, do they,
beloved, glow white-hot

against your skin, you can tell us,
you can tell us anything. She replies, *no of course not,*
what do you think this is,

a necklace of tongues?

10

A Thrill

for J.E.

and as you finish your cigarette
thinking *god when is something finally*
going to happen in this town
where even your exhaled smoke
seems to cling to the still air

his mossy hand is already gripping
the chair opposite and you nod
for him to sit. What covers his body
and face is a thick green layer
of dry grass. *Is this*

an art thing? you ask. He shrugs,
rustling like the air inside a conch.
Nobody else is making a fuss,
so you don't. There's so much grass
you can't see any skin, only

the mushroomy whites surrounding
the dark bark-brown of his eyes
and, when he yawns, the delicate,
intimate kittenpaw pink
of his wet mouth. He leans in,

palms flat on the table. *They've done*
an excellent job, you think:
you really can't see any skin at all.
The smell is dead leaves, snails,
sweet tree sap. *I get a real thrill,*

he whispers, *from chasing people.*
Leans back, two grainy brown handprints
either side of your coffee cup.
He looks at you and blinks slowly.
You stand up. He stands up.

The Tremendous Legislator Has Insisted That Everything Be An Indescribable Shade Of Purple He Dreamed Once

He keeps batting the swatches from the hands of the interior designers,
yelling *NO I mean much purpler than that* or *NO that's too fucking purple*.
We've brought Him alpine asters and violets and irises and lavender
and aubergines and cauliflowers and purple carrots but it's none of those.

We flew in the world's foremost expert on purple from a foreign university
and she talked with Him for hours about the science of purple, after which
He said, *you know, it's just that when I see that purple in my dreams,
it just makes me feel so happy. So can you help me or not?*

She paused and said *did you know the only word in the English language
that rhymes with purple is 'cirple', an archaic Scottish term for
a horse's arse*, and then there was a long pause where we were silently
willing her to blink, but she didn't and His top lip twitched

and the antique clock ticked like a glacier, and then of course her return flight
hit a mountain, so that was a whole new nation imposing sanctions.
Someone suggested that maybe our finest neurologists could invent a machine
that allowed us to film His dreams, so we could see the shade of purple too,

and of course He loved that, because He doesn't know our finest neurologists
are all dead or in exile, and that when He visits the labs it's mostly
just pensioners we've dressed up in white coats, aimlessly
shoving electrodes into the skulls of their unlucky spouses.

So then instead we had to enlist our tenth finest avant-garde film director
to help us make a fake dream machine, which He was visibly excited by
when He sat down to watch the footage, but within minutes He was shouting
these are not my dreams and anyway nothing here is purple

and smashing the machine to bits with His father's golf clubs. So now
we're hoping He eventually just moves onto something else,
because when He says He wants everything to be this shade of purple,
He really does mean everything: the palace decor, army uniforms, the flag,

the currency, everybody's hats and underwear, all stray dogs, everything.
We're slipping strong cheese in his late-night snacks in the hope
of turning His dreams into nightmares, which, now we think about it,
might cause more problems than it solves, in the long run.

Little Sociopath Attends The Wedding Reception Of A Distant Relative

Sophie and Jon Sophie and Jon Sophie and Jon Sophie and Jon
he hisses a low volume, baring his teeth like a luchador.
They wait for the photographer to finish arranging the groom's
many ham-faced uni mates. Some children would be adorable
in waistcoat and tails and such shiny black shoes, but he just looks
like a little bank manager. A server with a silver platter offers him
a mushroom vol-au-vent; he snatches five and crams them in
all at once, chewing with his mouth wide open and shouting
mmmuffrooms i love muffrooms!

During the speeches, at the table furthest from the couple,
he grabs a rubbery chicken breast from a neighbour's plate
and revs it up and down like a toy car,
leaving brown gravy trails all over the tablecloth. During the disco,
the other children dance in the red and green flashing lights, while he
sneaks around by himself in the car park. His favourite moment of the night
is watching a groomsman puking behind a red Mondeo.

Across a full double-page of the well-wishers' signing-in book,
somebody has scrawled *hop u get a divorce, u pair of assholes*
which somebody else has made an ineffective attempt at scribbling out.

At The Park, A Grown Man Has Got His Head Caught In The Railings

Possibly somebody loves,
or at some point has loved,
this man. But it's hard to imagine
right now. It's hard to imagine
that for most of his life
he hasn't been stuck
at this ninety-degree angle,
fists flailing, jeans sagging
at the waist. He's so angry
with the railings,
with the soft mud under his boots
and especially with the teenagers
who are laughing at him
from the picnic benches.

You could empty a whole tub
of vegetable oil onto his neck
and tug him out by his belt loops
but he wouldn't thank you for it.
And of course you can't ask him
what he was trying to do
in the first place.
He doesn't know
what his pain looks like
from the outside.

If You Want To Make Sense Of The Greatest Love Songs Ever Written

picture them as monologues delivered by a man in a parked car,
roaring the words into the sealed ear of an undressed mannequin
The mannequin is in the driving seat and the man is in the back.

No mannequin, of course, has need for nipples but somebody,
most likely the man himself, will have drawn them on.
The words may not be sung. *You mean the world to me,* he'll shout,

I know I've found in you my endless love. Nobody will be around
but if they are, from outside the car it should sound like
an entirely one-sided argument, the voice muffled and the words unclear.

The man may not alter any gender pronouns. *Baby,* he'll shout,
my baby don't care for shows, and he don't even care for clothes,
he cares for me. The man must not weep as he shouts: the mannequin

mustn't be a stand-in for a real or former flesh-and-blood lover.
The mannequin stands only for itself. Similarly, the man
may not be one of those people who falls in love with inanimate objects

like trucks or Eiffel towers: no, he must know the mannequin is a mannequin
and still run his fingers through its hair from behind
with the detached and expert bearing of lonely and long-fingered ostler.

It will be autumn, night, a dry wind disturbing the carpark's damp litter,
a supermarket's green neon reflected in the puddles.
I want to know what love is, he'll bellow, *I know you can show me.*

I Am So Angry With You For Bringing This Here

See the polite little angel cakes
and mini-quiches the others brought,
all queueing on their trestle tables;
the taffeta and the silk, the candlelight,
the handsome banner reading
Congratulations Sophie And Jon: all this
and you decide to contribute a sow's bladder
stuffed with lard, still in its semi-transparent carrier bag.
They're all pretending it's not there,
stench of rust and old sex, but look at the way
their lips purse, look at the way the bag clings
to the scrubbed pink blush of its curvature;
they're suspicious that even touching the outside of the plastic
would make their fingers somehow come away sticky.
Even the guests who weren't yet here
to see you sashay in with it
and plop it right on top of the sandwiches,
even they know it was you who brought it,
because who else would have?
It's not even cooked properly
because you didn't listen properly
to the butcher's instructions.
There's pig's blood on your new shoes
and you have let everybody down.
Kiss me, hard, with tongues. I love you.

An Otherwise Uneventful Holiday

The kid has somehow got hold of a jellyfish
and starts cramming it into a jam jar
but so carefully, so tenderly
it doesn't even sting him
and for a moment, we stop
because where did he get this touch,
these fingers of a master sushi chef,
easing that delicate translucence
into its not quite big enough space
and the circling seabirds fall silent
and the waves hush and then
it's our fault, because we
shout his name, and he flinches
and one of the stinging fronds
still trailing from the jam jar
flexes, and grazes his cheek,
his lovely soft marshmallow cheek,
and the red welt blooms like a curse,
like a line in the sand,

and then it's the sound of a kid
trying his hardest to stop screaming
as he brings jam jar lid to jam jar
just as the jellyfish, as though it knows,
pulls in its fronds
like fingers avoiding a slamming door
and he screws the lid on tight
and before we can reach him
he hurls the jar out to sea, high,
the throw of his life,
and at the top of its arc
the sun explodes through it
and of course our arms are by now
around the kid, of course they are,

but don't blame us also for looking past him,
for trying to locate the spot in the Aegean
where the tiny splash
has already composed itself
as though nothing had ever disturbed it.

On A Spring Morning In April, The Newspaper Editor Makes Cupcakes With His Beautiful Son

> *Rescue boats? I'd use gunships to stop migrants*
> *The Sun newspaper*

His beautiful wife is still in bed,
stretching her limbs on soft linen.
His beautiful son mispronounces ingredients adorably.
These people are like cockroaches.

Elsewhere on quiet dinghies
skin squeaks across hot rubber.
these people look out across the expanse of ocean
and sunlight strikes the surface like a benediction.
These people look how to cross the expansive ocean.

He has a double first in English Literature. Every day on the train
on the way to the office, he is able
to read great works of literature. One day Sophocles
one day Zora Neale Hurston.
That he believes reading great works of literature encourages empathy
is not in question.
That he loves his beautiful wife is not in question.
That he loves his beautiful son is not in question.
That he is loved by his own parents,
that his own parents held aspirations for him,
many of which he has already achieved,
is not in question.
He nuzzles his nose into his child's hair.

My wife is a better person than I am, he chuckles at dinner parties.
My son has made me a better person than I was.

The sunlight floods the edges of the blinds.
His beautiful son's little fingers crinkle around the spoon.

I would loose the gunships upon them
The sunlight swarms the edges of the blinds.

Sometimes the terrible things you do
can spoil the lining of the skintight wetsuit of the self
like poorly-stashed cigarette packets. Sometimes the terrible things you do
are too big to reside inside the lightweight one-man tent of the self
without irreparably distending the fabric,
and sometimes the terrible things you do just yawn
like sunned cats on windowledges,
dissolve like icing sugar in warm water.

His beautiful son is not allowed to put the cupcakes in the oven
or take them out of the oven.
These people are spreading like norovirus.
He does not want to risk his son's fingers
on the hot metal of the baking tray.
His desire to keep his child's beautiful blank skin unblemished
is not in question

and he tidied up the spelling and grammar
and the presses fired up and the plastic wrapped bundles landed
in all the newsagents and supermarkets and petrol stations.

When, in the night, his beautiful son worries about monsters,
he tells his son monsters do not exist

The Tremendous Legislator Had A Wonderful Sense Of Humour

like when He would visit the capital's one remaining hospital
and seek out some old man standing by the bed of some dying wife
and first of all show kindness, perhaps embracing the old man
or even lifting a beaker of water to the woman's dry lips,
and then He would take the old man outside the room and say,
lightly, as though it were just occurring to Him for the first time,
wouldn't it be funny, old man, if you told her you'd never really loved her?
and the two bodyguards behind him would just shift their weight slightly,
and they would follow the old man back in and listen as he explained
that every second of their many years together had been a lie
and that almost every day he had fantasised his hands around her neck.
Sometimes the old woman would die to the sound of Presidential giggling
and other times He would wait long hours before allowing the old man
to reassure her that it was all just a joke, all just a practical joke.

Occasionally, rarely, an old man would refuse, clamp his jaw shut
and receive such a thrashing from the bodyguards
that, after, the wife would be forced to shuffle over on her deathbed
to let him crawl in beside her like an exhausted newlywed. Those times,
back in His motorcade, He would wipe away a sentimental tear
and reflect out loud on the impressive stubborn power of real love,
even as His hands shook with rage at the disobedience of it,
even as He looked up the addresses of the old couple's grownup children.

Trucks

I need to be somewhere I can watch trucks
from above. To stand at a top-floor window
in a hotel near the airport
and hurl imaginary harpoons
at their chrome skulls. I need to topple
their dumb and capable squareness,
to drag them sideways in a shower of sparks
and haul them in like Archelus Hammond of Nantucket,
the first sailor ever to kill a sperm whale and christen it
for the creamy oil that pooled from its brow.
I need to feel the crunch of metal and glass
between my canine teeth.

I need to lean over the rail
of a motorway footbridge
on a still day just before rush hour,
to conduct the cars, move them where I need them
before they reach the bottom line at my feet.
I need to rotate them and sort them
like Linus Jorenbo of Stockholm,
the first winner of the European Tetris Championship.
And the trucks. I need the trucks to keep coming
for ever, drifting in from the vanishing point
like an endless supply of those long thin blocks
you always need but never get, not in the real game,
not until it's already too late.

Lobsters Make Noise Like Violins

Man with lobster trap on head,
your sunburnt face is crisscrossed
pink and white. The chafing at your neck
where rust borders skin
looks a little raw.   You shouldn't pick at it.

Man with lobster trap on head,
don't you ever take it off? I've seen you
using an old skewer to poke morsels
through the grille. How do you sleep?

Man with lobster trap on head,
are you a lobster trap enthusiast?
Yours, with its arched frontage
and horizontal wooden slats down the side
is a classic New England lobster trap.
Did you know that already, or
don't you really care about all the different types?

Man with lobster trap on head,
are you doing it to feel lobsterish? Your teeth
chatter like the scuttle of chitin,
your breath is sour as gull farts.
You might mate for life
if anyone would have you.

Clever, man with lobster trap on head,
to turn cage into exoskeleton,
but how did it come to this, and
when did you loft it like a trophy
and decide to stop, forever, being
boy with nothing at all on head?

It's really not fair of you,
man with lobster trap on head,
to keep shrieking so much:
everyone knows that's only air escaping.

The Tremendous Legislator's Second Most Accurate Body Double Is Torn To Pieces Attempting To Flee The City

Tear him to pieces. He's a conspirator.

--Julius Caesar, Act III Scene III

The older one, the former actor;
who was always too good looking, really.
And as with all of these things, it's chance:
his hood blown back by a gust of wind
just as he passes an electronics shop
with twenty televisions all broadcasting
news of the coup. He watches the public
convene in that greasy light, and shrugs.
Twenty-odd good years, a lifestyle
better by far than most. Fresh fruit
whenever he wanted it. *Who are you?*
one shouts. *Where are you going?*
Some of the screens descend into static.

He projects his voice all the way to the back:
I am Cinna the Poet, I am Cinna the Poet.
Nobody gets the reference. Their mucky fingers
break him like bread.
He doesn't know how long it should take
for him to die, but this feels like too long.
Right at the end, he thinks he hears
a woman yell *tear him for his bad verses*
and he is almost grateful. To die smiling
is no bad death, in these times. She will end up
stashing a metacarpal in her purse,
which she will pass on to her children
and grandchildren, to keep on their mantelpieces.

These Are The Things You Can Do When You Sneak Into The Old Ice-Cream Factory Alone, After Midnight

Spend several hours standing very still,
listening carefully for disembodied laughter
and where it may be coming from.

Break into the storeroom and gather handfuls
of stale peanut sprinkles to throw
at the employee-of-the-month photographs.

Run your flat palm gently over the cold flanks
of the giant stainless-steel mixing cylinders
still and stabled like denatured ruminants.

On the way out, stop at the toilets
where you'll find a ragged but reassuringly wide gloryhole
in the wall of the far-end cubicle.

Crouch down and put your eye to the hole.
Why not? The floor is no dirtier than your own bathroom,
if it's your jeans you're worried about.

Don't be such a baby. Hey, imagine if,
when you did it,
there was another eye staring back at you,

wide to the whites in terror, and a voice whispering
help me, help me, please help me.
Obviously there won't be. You're the only one here.

The Tremendous Legislator Has Taken To Sniffing Petrol

It's just you and him left alive in the bunker.
There are about thirty thousand calories
in a gallon of gasoline, he keeps saying,
enough to power a person for twenty days.
We ran out of powdered egg this morning.
Despite it all, you're still impressed
at his continued command of esoteric facts.
It's one of the traits you've always admired in him.
Your favourite is the one about the hummingbird:

asking him to repeat it has been a surefire antidote
to the blues, these last months. *A drop of nicotine*
the size of a matchhead is enough
to kill a hummingbird. He knows this for sure
because had his labs find out the exact amount.
You went down there once: they move
more like dragonflies than birds. Even caged,
they flit. You remember the neat lines of lifeless bodies
arranged on the workbenches like adorable sunbathers.

You want to ask him *Gasoline? You don't wish that you*
were a car, do you, ha ha? but you're concerned
he won't take that sort of levity very well.
You only joined in the once. The walls of the bunker
shimmered and your eyes felt too far from your feet.
It makes your mind big enough to, at last,
hold your genius, he told you, and now the idea
of stopping him makes you want to cry.
The petrol is in a plastic washing up bowl.

He hunches over it with a pillowcase over his head.
He's getting a red rash around his mouth and nostrils.

The Moment When The Tremendous Legislator Should've Known The Jig Was Up

Bored, He orders strawberries.
They know by now He takes them chilled
on porcelain. Exactly twelve,
no cream, no sugar, halved lengthways,
all traces of green removed,
none bigger than a kitten's fist.

The servants and advisors
sit at desks answering emails.
Nobody moves. It's not mutiny,
He doesn't think, but apathy.
He repeats the order. When He gets them,
they taste just as good as usual.

Branch

After "Broken Fall" by Bas Jan Ader

The man dangling from the branch
looks like a young Johann Cruyff.
When you ask if he needs your help,
he says *no don't worry, I do this often.*
When you ask *how often* he says
probably once a year. He looks
so much like a young Johann Cruyff
that his English accent surprises you.
As though he has read your mind,
he starts bicycling his legs midair,
making imaginary elegant passes,
sidefoot, cross-field. He hurdles
an imaginary late slide tackle from
an imaginary German fullback.
The branch, thinner than his ankle,
jounces like a novelty rubber pencil.
It's not so high that a fall would kill him,
but the stream underneath seems
shin-jarringly shallow. *Is the stream
not too shallow for this?* you ask.
He says *I'm not telling you.* You ask
why do you do this once a year?
There is a pause. He stops kicking.
It's no worse than a birthday party.
He starts again. His arms
must be getting tired. You turn away.
My arms are getting tired, he yells.
It's obvious what's going to happen.
You put your earbuds back in
so you won't even hear any splash.
If you want to see it,
you can always come back next year.

The Tremendous Legislator's Head Is Put On Display By The New Regime

Soap, wax, ice, uncooked mince, turnips, shit:
our underground artists had grown so skilled at the effigies,
dragging his stern essence
through any material they could find,

that when we saw the real thing, real,
on its plain table, it was so hard to believe,
even when we queued like a bank run
to ignore the *Do Not Touch* signs

and pinch its raw cheeks, tug its dead beard.
We cradled it in our elbow nooks, selfied Pietas,
pushed its grey lips to our exposed nipples,
even the men. We held it up to our ears like a radio

to take its whispered sightless commentaries
for our own secret wishes. We squeezed
its temples and shook it like a moneybox,
disappointed at the lack of rattle.

We were irrepressible in those days; the low jumble
of our chatter growing louder the nearer we got:
those closest whooped, chanted, sang.
As soon as our turns were over, we sprinted round the back

to get in line again. It couldn't last.
They tried refrigeration, then fumigation,
then noseplugs, then rubber gloves, but we couldn't halt
its slow spoil. The worst of us brought spoons.

We stopped only when he was a dark stain
spread like a placemat, deep in the wood of the table.
The skull, we must've mothballed. Who cares about a skull?
A skull might just as well have been anybody.

Rat Centipede

Don't look so worried about the rat centipede:
he will, for the most part, remain in plain sight.
He's made of three and a half rats but the front and back
are the same rat. We felt that was important.
I don't think any of us expected him to live this long.

At night we tuck our bedsheets into our mattresses
and our pyjama bottoms into our bedsocks
and give him free run of the place. He climbs the walls
and the skitter of his many toes soothes us to sleep
like soft rain on tin. Please be considerate:
he reacts poorly to sudden movements and just like all of us
he doesn't seem to have any clear idea what he is for.

Of course, he's driving the local cats crazy; they tap at the windows,
desperate to unpick his delicate stitching and uncover
the four delectable little hearts beating inside.

These Three Young Ladies Have Come All The Way From Australia

says the compere. They wear
matching white vests and knickers
and they are jumping up and down on the spot,
holding hands. At first the room is silent enough
to hear the metronomic thumps, the soft kisses
of bare feet parting from beery stageboards
but after five minutes people are quietly
resuming conversation. After ten,
some get up to visit the bar or toilet
and after fifteen there is some heckling,
even booing. On twenty-four minutes,
the young lady in the middle stops
because her nose is bleeding.
Her colleagues on both sides continue to jump
and she grips their hands as the blood
channels the corners of her wide smile,
down her chin, between her breasts.
On twenty-eight minutes, the noses
of the other two young ladies follow suit
simultaneously and explosively,
splattering the tables at the front.
Out of breath, vests stained red,
the young ladies bow at the waist. The blood
plumblines from their nostrils and pools at their feet.
They exit stage right.

Acknowledgements:

The Little Robot Who Makes You Relax was published in Interpreters House; *Branch, A Thrill* and *The Tremendous Legislator's Head Is Put On Display* were all published in separate issues of Magma; *Trucks* was published in Bare Fiction; *The Tremendous Legislator Had A Wonderful Sense Of Humour* was published in Butcher's Dog; *The Tremendous Legislator Has Taken To Sniffing Petrol* was published in Strix; *These Three Young Ladies...* was published in New Welsh Review and Highly Commended in the Forward Prize.

I am, as always, extremely grateful to Anna Nelson, who is always the first critical reader of my work, and Martin Kratz, who is invariably the second. I'm extremely lucky to have your input: these poems are better for it. Secondly, a huge thank you to Colin Bancroft: I'm honoured to be a part of Nine Pens. Many thanks to Ian Humphreys and Faith Lawrence, who provided excellent advice on some of these poems, as well as some much-needed Zoom camaraderie during the slog of lockdown. In a similar vein, thanks also to Sarah Mosedale, Liz Aiken, Becky Field, Susan Earlam and Hannah Whiteoak, who are excellent at helping me decide whether I'm writing poetry or prose, and to Eli Regan for co-hosting so many brilliant North-West literary nights with The Other. Many thanks to John England for providing the inspiration for 'A Thrill. I'm also grateful to my colleagues in the English department at Runshaw College, and to my English Literature and Combined students, for allowing me to have a job where I get to talk about poetry with clever people most days. Finally, to my parents, for their unconditional love and support.